Community Helpers

Veterinarians

by Cari Meister

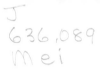

Bullfrog
Books

Ideas for Parents and Teachers

Bullfrog Books let children practice reading informational text at the earliest reading levels. Repetition, familiar words, and photo labels support early readers.

Before Reading
- Discuss the cover photo. What does it tell them?
- Look at the picture glossary together. Read and discuss the words.

Read the Book
- "Walk" through the book and look at the photos. Let the child ask questions. Point out the photo labels.
- Read the book to the child, or have him or her read independently.

After Reading
- Prompt the child to think more. Ask: Do you have a pet? Do you have to take it to the vet? What other things do vets do for animals?

Bullfrog Books are published by Jump!
5357 Penn Avenue South
Minneapolis, MN 55419
www.jumplibrary.com

Library of Congress Cataloging-in-Publication Data
Meister, Cari, author.
  Veterinarians / by Cari Meister.
    pages cm.—(Community helpers)
  Summary: "This photo-illustrated book for early readers describes what veterinarians do to help keep all kinds of animals healthy, including dogs, cats, zoo animals, and farm animals"—Provided by publisher.
  Audience: Ages 5-8.
  Audience: K to grade 3.
  Includes bibliographical references and index.
  ISBN 978-1-62031-096-0 (hardcover)
  ISBN 978-1-62496-163-2 (ebook)
  ISBN 978-1-62031-140-0 (paperback)
  1. Veterinarians—Juvenile literature. 2. Veterinary medicine—Juvenile literature. I. Title.
  SF756.M45 2015
  636.089092—dc23

                         2013044267

Editor: Wendy Dieker
Series Designer: Ellen Huber
Book Designer: Lindaanne Donohoe
Photo Researcher: Kurtis Kinneman

Photo Credits: All photos by Shutterstock except: Alamy/ZUMA Press, Inc., 14–15; Alamy, 23; iStockPhoto, 6, 18, 21; Superstock, cover, 4, 5, 8–9, 16–17

Printed in the United States of America at Corporate Graphics, North Mankato, Minnesota.
6-2014
10 9 8 7 6 5 4 3 2 1

Table of Contents

All Kinds of Vets 4

At the Vet Clinic 22

Picture Glossary 23

Index 24

To Learn More 24

All Kinds of Vets

Ava wants to be a veterinarian.

What do they do?

5

They care for sick animals.

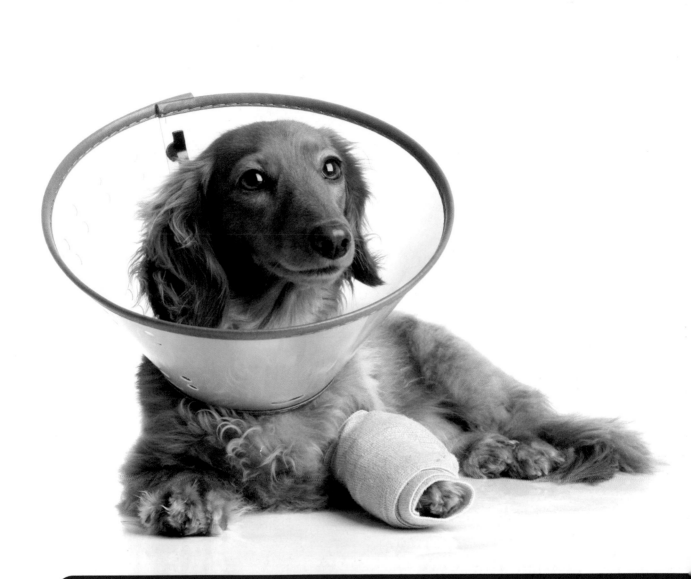

They help animals that are hurt.

They help animals
stay well.

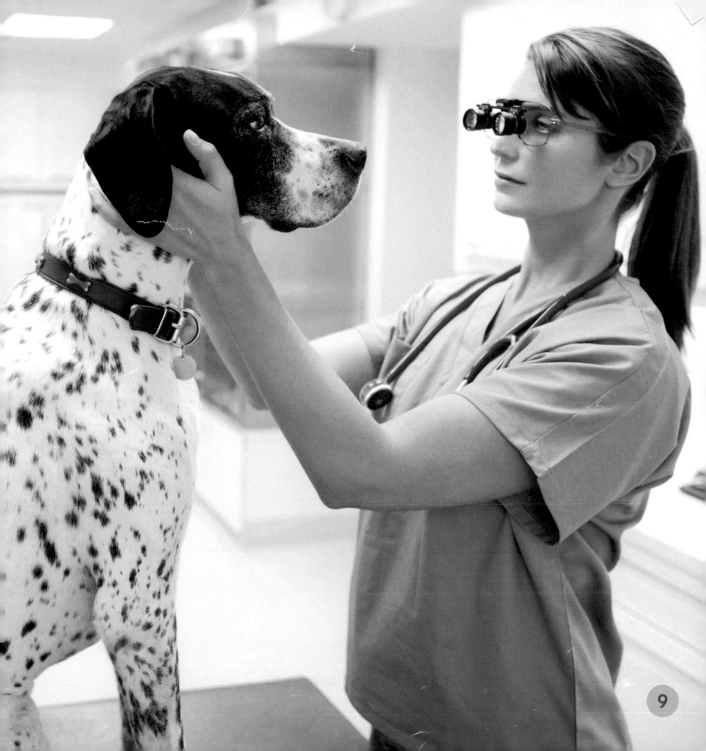

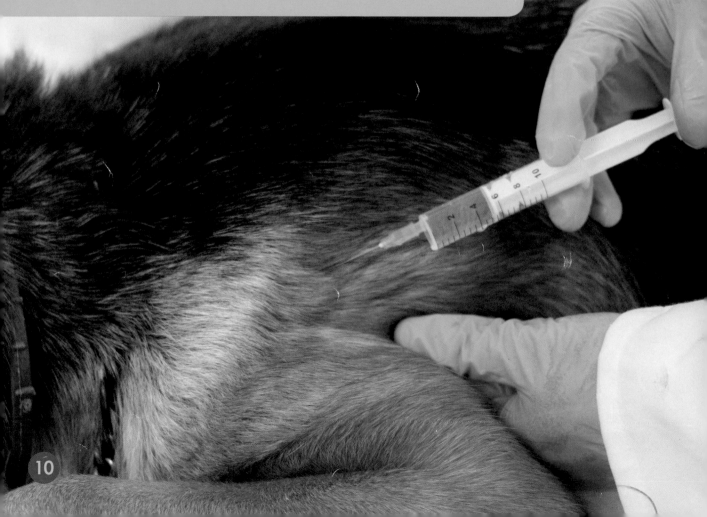

Max needs a check-up.
Dr. Green gives him shots.
Ouch!

But now he might not get sick.

Oh no!
Milo got hit
by a car.

Dr. Hill looks
at the x-ray.

She fixes his leg.

Dr. May is at a zoo.

Raj needs surgery.

She cares for him.

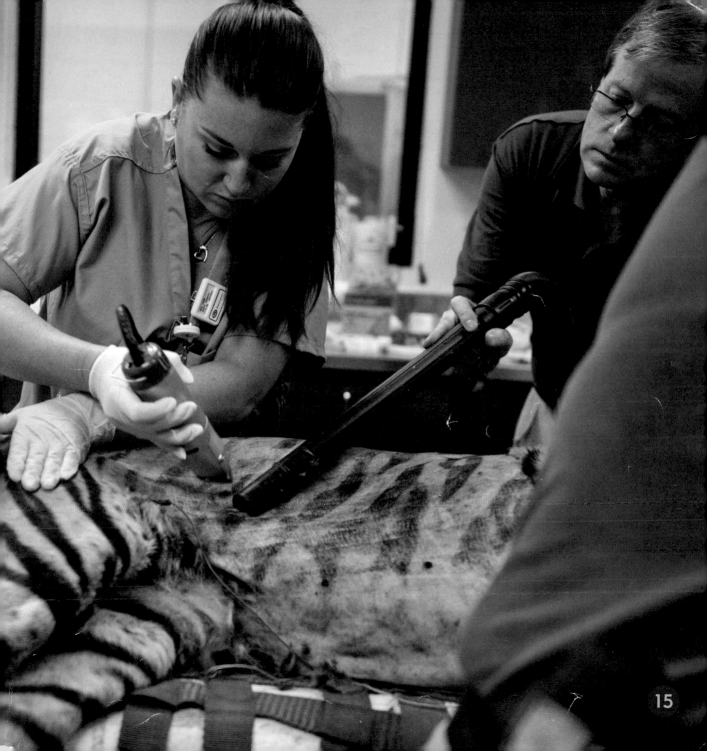

Dr. Wu works at an aquarium. A shark is sick. He needs medicine. Get well!

Dr. Soo cares for horses.
Polly is having a foal.
Dr. Soo helps.

foal

Vets do good work!

At the Vet Clinic

monitor
Vets watch an animal's heartbeat and other information on this screen.

light box
A box that lights up so vets can look at x-rays.

exam table
Animals sit or lie on the table so vets can check them out.

Picture Glossary

aquarium
A place where people can study and watch animals that live in water.

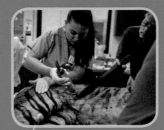

surgery
When a vet needs to cut into an animal's body to fix a problem inside.

foal
A baby horse.

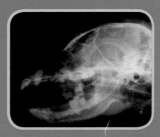

x-ray
A picture of an animal's or person's bones.

Index

aquarium 17

car 13

foal 18

hurt 7

medicine 17

shots 10

sick 6, 11, 17

surgery 14

x-ray 13

zoo 14

To Learn More

Learning more is as easy as 1, 2, 3.

1) Go to www.factsurfer.com

2) Enter "vets" into the search box.

3) Click the "Surf" button to see a list of websites.

With factsurfer.com, finding more information is just a click away.